To Burn in Torturous Algorithms

To Burn in Tortuous Algorithms

Heath Brougher

And, thus, the Spiral begins...

To Burn in Torturous Algorithms
Heath Brougher

© 2017 Heath Brougher
Front Cover art, "The Red Infinity of Spin," by Daniel Y. Harris
Back Cover art, "Wormhole Series: The Convenience of
Modernity," by Daniel Y. Harris

ISBN-13: 978-0692055441

Weasel Press
Manvel, TX
http://www.weaselpress.com

Printed in the U.S.A.

TABLE OF CONTENTS

Dedication

The People to whom this book is dedicated are not so vain as to need their names mentioned for all to see. They know who they are.

Brief Explanation of Spiralism

Although I have been writing my entire life, I did not begin to submit my "life's work" for publication until three years ago at the age of thirty-four. I've already published three chapbooks and one full length book although THIS book will never fall below the second most important book I will ever publish during my writing career. I say this because this book introduces the masses to a writing style I began to develop as far back as seventeen years old and which I have termed Spiralism. It was originally called Auraism but, after the past few years, Spiralism started to sound better. This first book wades the reader into what Spiralism is and gives them a of glimpse of and a hint at what Spiralism can and will evolve into over the years. It is a chaotic mixture of random image and thought, all held together with semi-colons. Just remember, this is the beginning of the Spiral. Who knows just what it could Spiral into and temporarily become? Enjoy this book and begin your own Spirals. Maybe even try writing your own Spiralism and see how it evolves through the years.

The Vulture's Grandiosity

Under the slime of sky
filthy things acrawl; american fangs
drip with venom; the learning enemy
slowly catching on thoughtwise;
antagonist for hire— it won't
be hard to find one, maybe
the supra everyman in this land
of resurgent malaria and silken guillotines;
such chryselephantine thoughts cut down
by the Patriot Axe halfswung by
robotic religion across the neckless roads
in the deadcold of night— the rose at midnight
bleeding beneath the luminiferous ether;

a nation suffering from McDonald's Syndrome;
bloated; limped amuck; gone kindleburning, bookburning;
just like an assembly line—
the fleshen Patriot Axe cuts down again
on our open-eyed thoughts—
never hearing of a recent Buddhist battlefield not sparked by white men
the supra hands, the mangled populace,
hypocritical and imperialistic as all in nature, in evolution,
sing out in unison "Let Free Dumb Ring!"
left to their profligate materialism, their favorite distraction,
the new american pastime; they wash their brains
in the cable news basin, receiving their opinions;

Applepicker's Disease

Nightsickness is upon the weather
again— early darkness blooms out
growing deeper night after night;
circular death-irises continue
to swoop and swirl in the wind
as the barelyalive dried-up carcasses
of severed deadveined leaves flit
along the hard, solid ground of Fall's
predictable mutation into Winter;

sundowns and nothingnesses straight ahead;

pulled puppyteeth stain alabaster carpets
with russet blotches— I knew,
and I still know, of the emptiness
of us all— eventual bone then sand and dust;

the haunted hospitals; the general
failings of quality; this is the downslope
of a rollercoaster; my head is lodged forever
at the Brokensoul Inn—
but I know what I know and I know
that I am not Joseph Stalin
or an Iodine God;

A Man Named Child

I once had a way in through the side door;
there are no more yellow noons; sloth and slug;
bombs made of sharp bones are kept
in the house made of fragile marrow;
the best of my bliss was crude bliss at best;
I'll die my death hopefully slowly—
it's what I deserve [all those I have forsaken];
may my big baby brother remove me
from this prominent permafrost of the mind?—

born into a suburban world of blonde on blonde violence
and the snobben pseudorich—

you spoke of Eve's ribcage;
I was the town drunk of the Endless Summer
of the first summer of the Millennium;
moonshine brandishing bright as the most lucent moon—
bright as the luminous multitude of Epiphanies
that were to come to me, through my suffering, years later;
thoughts of our common duality and poetic mindrot;
or Manmade and Universal realities;
all here, all had under the sky mostly blocked
by the of branches of anemic suburban trees;

Severed from the Mainstream Thought

When I'm an old man—
[if I ever get there]
I'd like to sit on my front porch
and have all this;
this is; all this is;
and have the passerby younglings
comment that there sits
a sapient old man; must
know a lot; and all the while I'd
be reiterating in my mind
what Burroughs wrote so many years before,
the day before he died—
"there is no final enough of wisdom";

hazydusty my mind still achurn;
a whole life spent in the mistiness of thought—
endless ruminations leading down
so many different pathways;
joy a thing unknown
in a life of constant pensiveness;

looking for answers; all there is;

in life one must choose between
seeking happiness or Truth—
the majority reach for happiness—
most without even knowing there was a choice;

I have chosen to seek the Truth,
that long-suffered Causeway;

Chickenpox at the Slaughterhouse

My mouthy spirit suddenly spins off-hinge
and decries with such anger and frustration
the idioms and idiots abound; the fatalism
of America brings with it a beaucoup of smashed-thought
in this ersatz democracy; the Illusioner's diversion
grows more so every day keeping us on the same page— the remote control:
the one last freedom of choice you really have
and always stuck on the station that airs
The Menstrual Cycles of the Rich and Famous;
pathetic heart of heavy human being;
I'll tell you the Truth— don't get with the pogrom [or the program]
like you're being told— I say let's make this
the Rulemaker's Reckoning— let's turn on the brain
until we have at last the billionth skeptic
and we'll eat of the giant marshmallows of the sky
and spray wave after wave of liquid flame
upon the Wrongwingers; Everywingers; we'll be a wingless bird still afly
in this troubled atmosphere; with the flowers on fire
we'll cut away the misaction potential and bask in my mouthy silence;
accept only jonquils while bathing in the overindulgent blood;
having at last the sound of heavily distorted guitar feedback;

Year of the Pinata

The English is sprinkled with rolling tongue,
weaving incoherent clothes— a season
of nonsense is born and welcomed—
a respite from the cold drab of December noons;
hung from a string in the middle of the den,
its ribs bore sweetness as we swung,
alive in the lamplight breathing
bigger breath than before; it kept
chiming in, shattering the *silencio*—
the world and its words were vague,
faint to the grasp, yet we were suddenly
peppered with vibrant energy; we wanted
this time to carry on; swinging to and fro
in all its motley glory, we whacked
and whacked; blooming in broken English;
we stuttered and danced blindfolded
in front of the widest of opened eyes; swung and whacked
and swung and whacked again,
and when the bowel was broken and the cardboard rhino
leaked its plethora of sweetness onto the floor
we knelt down and gorged upon the belly's plenty;

Summer's Mechanical Symphony

Fading in; fading out; lawnmower raging in July past my window
around the neighborhood; chopping blades with blades;
grassblades with metalblades; early morning thunder on the ground
wisps through my window—

I notice the scent of a broken fragrance; of bleeding grass;
the headless grassblades; shorn green tendrils
mixed with the dew awaken me from my early morning slumber
to hear the mechanical storm raging in the yards below;
the butchers and their grasskillers pacing; fading in;
fading out; down the yards; around the houses;
binging on oil and gas to guillotine the dewy tendrils of summer;

The United States of Anhedonia

Plaintowns, plaincities, talking in
boring sentences; the banality of postmodern
American society; only thing exciting
is the fear caught from the tv;
the dailygrind grinding away the life;
the weeks, months, years, ground-down
into tiny pieces that, when assembled,
make up an entire life spent wasted by trivial routine;
largeportions of that life hang in heavy boredom,
day after day; ennui drifts throughout
the doldrums of these plaintowns, plaincities
yawning in the eternal forecast of reigning tedium;
the only smallcure for this lethargic monotony
is the omnipresent shoppingmalls that besmudge
the landscape of these plaintowns, plaincities—
an ugly motley flashing among the lassitudinal weariness
permeating the lazy air of these pococurantist plaintowns, plaincities,
giving brief respite from the otherwise jaded fatigue
that runs through the veins of the day;
that consumes the lives livingout so dull and flat
in these sleepy plaintowns, plaincities;
all the colors of the mind so monotone in these societies;
so lifeless, as if in a permanent winter;
brown and drab clothing; it's almost as if these plaintowns, plaincities
don't even wish for a bloomingup of vivacity;
as if they'd rather coughout and live their lives in
robotically scheduled and regimented segments;

The Beautiful Clusterfuck

All in jumble;
dissimilar pieces strewn together,
tangled veins and wires;
life lost and born;
today came loose at the seams;
after the tumult, it laid down
torn jagged remnants twisted
asleep together in a cluster;

a mountain of miscellaneous
piled far into the sky
looming motley in the shining sun;
things alive and things dead,
a haphazard landscape, yet somehow,
all the same [Dust] in the end,
and all a mangle of beauty;

Chade in Mina

You will eat your dinner of imitation crab meat
and generic sushi from the truck-stop; this roundtable
of concoctions and mixtures of toxic things mutate,
transform and transmogrify;
Manmade pollutants disturb the world,
rub nature the wrong way—

these defiled bones and guts and toxic toys
and food swing way off hinge and into the bizarre,
mutation after mutation—

"Momma my three legs; Dada my tenth neck;
Nana my vomiting up of overly-tampered-with chemicals?"

the extant Manmade dent in the Earth
has soaked deeply into the soil and sky;
mutated children or just plain dead babies everywhere;
this is the dying down; these are
the toxicology reports run amok
with unsafe chemicals— so where do we go from here?
just survive; try to live through
the enormity of it all— these poisons so deeply ingrained
in land, in air; a colossal intertwined coalescence of Manmade toxins;

there will be no easy fix,
no sudden magnanimous cure
to what we've wrought and taken
into our bodies and the Earth entire;

the toll of a mangled Earth rings loudly;

sickness
rises;

Gelatinous

Foodstove unused; no need;
fastfood reign supremely high;
foodstave infected with calorie and trans;
tired bodies; arms reach for the apple, its purity,

unattainable;

a quick morphing and is born
the gelatinous generation— laying stagnantly
in the chair; the weight of the world;
even blubberbones searching for health
can find none; no oasis; just chemical greasedrippings;
bodyfails; no movement; soured malnutrition
and human interference; trapped here
in this toxic cage; softerskin
and the arms are still reaching
for that apple,

unattainable;

Nuclear Baby

My mother was pregnant with me during the Three Mile Island crisis;
she, breathing contaminated air

while I was floating in the amniotic swimming pool of her belly;
she, living only a forty-minute drive from the power plant;

nuclear air swept into her lungs and spread to my tiny alien body;
her umbilical cord— a soft hypodermic needle injecting radiated air;

atomic nutrients straight into my buttonless belly;
I was born into a world of nuclear waste; tainted skies

and clouds pouring acid rain; venomous particles whisking along the toxic breeze;
I came nascent and pink into this world gasping for my first breath

among the poison that blew cold and mutagenic
along the air-paths of my hometown;

Bloodletting Go

Hush!; for it is just the blood letting go
of the vein; blood disembodied; extracted;
blood disemboweled; bloodstained streets and sidewalks;
the reddest of paint; the realest of rubicund
glimmering in the sun-jungles;

hush!; for the blood is no longer purple;
it has loosened and spilled from the peachblow aisles of the veins
into the air, onto the floor where it mingles
with oxygen; its shade ripening
to the ruddiest of reds; it has vacated
the velvetesque hallways of the body and bloomed
into a hue of solid primary vermillion
lying blatant; puddling before your very eyes;

Sarin Gas for the Soul

Human flesh and burning ventriloquists
among the Oxytocin addicts constantly
popping out more life for death by natural selection;
smug glob and hungry for heroin you bite
into the not human flesh of May's appleskin
as I say you'll always be in my hurt;

with thrushed throat you drink of the rubied Robitussin;
the jagged humanity of shiny toy landmines
and the jar of Immortality on the kitchen table
next to the machinegun; as you fall asleep you wonder
"are there assault rifles in heaven?" waking unto
the cleft, the cliff— two diverse
energies flowing at a simultaneous constant;

human flesh spouts its patriotism
[War's main catalyst [[not counting religion]]
not seeing the filth of the future, instead
raging against the Rulemaker's dominance
where we swim through oceans of teeth
and mansions of whores to pry the dagger
from cold dead hands; we eat not
of terror pie but of mint julep
in the fiery nights while the populace
are forever spun by the spin doctors;
not a true thought abound; mangled
by their smashmouthed words;
for We know that life is rain or shine;

all's quiet at the absent marketplace;
the professional bridgeburners down the road
rigging explosives so the bridge will tumble downward
like falling elevators and flaming lemmingdrops;
vile cakes of human flesh; bullets and babies;
big bloodclouds on the horizon;
tomorrow tickets go on sale for the extinction smackdab in america

24

where everything is never enough,
the rug never fully wrung dry;
the scent of sound then thinking forward to the present,
slouching toward ataxia day by day
as the clocksucker engulfs more time; soon
we'll have death guaranteed by american suffocation;
nine more years of winter; all the knives and molars in the world;
the entire heath, the vast wasteland;
america run amuck with cakesuckers
who waddle the sidewalks cracking the cement;
biting deeper into human flesh and thought;
incessant pantomimes of pensiveness;
the reality of postmodern bleeding;

we go suiciding as the tour guide shows us
the Kill-Yourself Collection deep into the overtone of night;
the scent of silence; nothingness; black
as a hole; not even stoneflowers bloom in this kingdom of endless Eclipse;
the jet-setters of white trash scalping tickets
to the extinction; I find it funny this human flesh has bloated
so much before it dies-off; crawls away
looking for a teacup's worth of water in the Grand Canyon
right before our self-inflicted meteor hits,
ripe with a dose of starvation;
poisoning ourselves every day; what else can be done
when the Annual Apathy Awards become a daily thing?
ghostshadows acned with acid scars scalp tickets
to the extinction;

ravenous masses of potential buyers wave handfuls of money;

Reunion

Years removed; coming back; reunion
happens; a dirty mouth
flounders in rust;

broken mothwings;

the body now more rotted,
we attend this Texas winter;

ages pass; sections of life
are come and gone— where
have I been?—

sitting in a thoughtless
braincysted seat; slithering in a dreamless
epileptic sleep; desperate among
the many fences; looking out;
half-blinded,
trying to feel my way back;

The January House Colossal

Morning pulse; the eye-colored dawn
was a hue we liked to thriving
yet a pale frozen orchard
spoke through chattering teeth
its bounty of ice; we wandered
at a pace low on sleep
through the aisles of fruit;
nibbling frozen berries— a hard candy
at the break of day; anew; ablaze;
weaving meekly through the driest air;
still half asleep; we wished
that winter would fade away
and turn our faces Springward;

Descent into Night

Candles burning dimmer;
shadowflickers; a ghost alive;
winter arrives, injecting the sky with gray;
bones commence their slow freeze;
I ramble about
thinking maybe of dragons;

Napalm Wig

A flammable gust kisses the neck of the woods
as pupils stare out from the upstairs
of the house of a Human Body where lunacy can be struck
instantly and bounce off the walls for hours,
especially when evening blooms and the moon
slightly peaks its silvery head out from the gathering gloaming;

the wind then thickens into a juice or jelly
of hot summer gales; scorching tempests
as the storm churns onward; ripening in foment;
raging in biting and burning whorls of fire;
running across czarina dresses, stealthily through unborn days,
like apricot shrubs that dance then don't;

Wordless

Low this morning
and don't feel
like saying words;

the rain speaks for me;
drizzletalk; drivel;
sapless darkgray sky;

there is no such thing as good venom;

Ripe as Postmodern Pain

If you are just lighting out for the territories, be careful,
for you'll find a little blood here, a little blood there;

in the back, pigs squeal with ripe pain
in this bloodshot butchershop;

various twisting aisles of severed skins
hang like jackal coats from the walls;

but those pig squealings in the back room
can still be heard and there is nothing to be done about it;

at least nothing other than a hope
for death to come on right quick;

don't go looking unless you are ready to dislike what you find;

Opus of the Opening Wounds

A million bones crushed;
this body removed; attenuated;
the minus body; scars for tattoos;
miles down the alleyway and still
the glass shrouds pierce; smashedbottle streets
and no glistening jaggedness to be seen
by these yellowed eyes; these pupils readjusting
to regular light; stale citywinds
ripple like claws dragged over the skin;
over the winter; now sick to the utmost;
brittleboned and nearly pulseless;

"Keep them sick but alive," said the doctor;
"sick but alive is where the money is";

Professional Suffering

You are not in the limedust, thankfully, as
the scrubbings of wind and a sniper from a land made of cake
await you and your family like a shadow shattered by a British-Brooklyn accent—

he is a recon man for the army of belly
dancers with machineguns and assault rifles—
more than just the thieves of your lunch money;

this strange-tongued person picked just for you, to place that
bullet where your lucky arachnoid braincyst won't block it
like the girl at the Texas theater shooting— shot in the head
and lived because the bullet hit a cyst on her brain she never even knew was there;

this is a dreamland dreamscape dreamscrape of the subconscious and skull
and throat and ional lions and invisible raindroppings
and dogs made of moths and the birds of Philadelphia—

look longwise into the future
you've been given a chance to attend
after Death tried so hard to envelop you in that rusty hospital;

The Deadbody Lights

The dead bodylights come;
shroud; what color are they?;
a glowing green?; a florescent blackness?; or
just darkness itself; a darkness alone?; does
stimulation or destimulation of the third eye cause
a whiteness or the appearance of that tunnel
with light at its end or am I scientifically mistaken?;
you find a tooth wrapped in a leaf;
everything eventually dissolves;
carbon billows outward;

A Nightmare in Purple

Down hollowest hill
a path twisted; born in the palm
of frigid gale; she wore a dress
that flowed through the fingers;
hard and high in the violets;
her face was a snapped-out-of-dream;
petite legs walking to the threshold
of a frightening wake;

Firewater Fiend

Priests in the Vatican Bar;
heavy with drink;
broken glass slides down drunken throat;
the snake slithers on;

woeful empty bottle; always plenty more;

play yourself— a nightly personal instrument—
head turns to vomit;
piles of torn access;
battling God all along the slippery way;
rampant puddles have pourn themselves;

evening continues; a man clothed in the devout;
cry that empty cry;
preconceived tantrum bites down on soft heads;
ears become bloodspouting relics of the awful sound;
you hide you face behind the flammable brown holy water;
pipes play the intoxicant endlessly forgiven;

all that's meek— those starved puppies
in a rainy street corner box
blurt out their torturesong
while your stomach feels warm
and ripe from that bitter Russian juice;

wolves and spies; saints and snakes
commingle; press thick ears
to thin walls; listening intently;
only to hear you swear to Drunk you're not God;

A Plushen World

At the helm of an aimless vessel;
twist contort and rise; trading
honey for kisses as we are hungry for kisses
laid to the lips— iffy, steering wild;
the no-stale thick liquid ooze
until we petrify
halfway up and down the atmosphere;
silverless dots nonexistence, the suiciders
have slat so may wrists, taken so may risks;
so we bleed like air bleeds when the air is bleeding;
at the helm of an aimless vessel,
twist contortion rise up to a yellow rose;
coming up contortion twists; silverless nonexistence nips
at the frozen blood halfway up the sky
we petrify and love these suicides;

Alice in Etherland

And lilylicked polyprose
heretical newfangler of fingernails
silentying the spacetalk phone
[there is so much just not
so much down here on this Earthly asphalt]
liverlived silentdream
occurs
accursing robbingstole all the appleblades
subwaying back to the Universe
on Broad St.
coughing among the metaltrain's
ricocheting speed
passing other stations
breezing
                              byfaces;

Broken Moonbone

Realburst, novaburst—
earlybird shoots the warm deer,
swallows the whisky; hair
of the dog who sunk
its teeth into your soul;

trauma-kit, bellyache—
the kite raping through the sky,
bladed, somehow razored, snipping
the twine of anything windblown its way;

evolution beats its chest
so apely day in, day out
as various roars of frustration
erupt in response to
a God that doesn't care;

Spin Now Around

A mark is made; one breath taken
and the entire world changed;
the constantly fluctuating structure
shifted at its heel; even one
baby's breath tilts and pulls, teeters
and pushes; all raveled in this rapture;

feelings bleed-out across colonies, countries,
invisible lines, arbitrary demarcations;
the pained and happy ones all the same;

that distant unmet girl blows away with dust;
energies released....
everything shifted, that clear dust clogging;
cloaking everything between what's perceivable
and not.... ruffles; waves; gnarled for the good; the bad;
the same;
(and we dare not mutter anything about light
or insect eyes, because we already have...
and paid for it with dead bodies);

Liquid Legs

Something less than solid;
submerged coils of drifting gas; upstream;
to the head; where the air is;
moving in waves, a shapeless gait,
obscured by the tang of blueberrywater; a velvet strawberry
iceflake dissolving; sugared; becoming;
onward motion; up ocean steps;
a skyghost of the water; bubbling;
exiting dankness with jostle;
something of sprint; immaculately contour-void;
removed of space; time; of place;
evanescent existence in pulp-form;
nevertheless strutting away; an exotic saunter
flowing whatever it flowed across the bodiless limbs;

A Husk of Evening

The milk drum beats
walking razor edges;
sun pales the red shingles above
leading to the massive fire of the heart;

repentance; old wilted trees
loom big in the yard; grass
so green; this return,
the chords, face the music;

these apples; foster children
of the sky; fall downward
to a flat brown end;
tonsils turn as the evening persists;
so buried in this tale of high;

no one is named here
in the fading warm limbo;

whispers of leaves and branches
take their turns being among;
decree nothing but what they know;
innocence battered again; waning music;
shafts of yellow glimmering little to none;

young mouth surrounds the beating breast;
night curdles over;

A Brief Respite for Remembrance

I heard the violin-voiced bird yesterday—
this means what it always means—   Springtime is on the
horizon—

the wind will wear warmth once again and the volume of the colors
of the valley will flood so verdantly ripe;

yes, this;   yes, this;

and I hear again a bird—   a china bird, their songs more melodic
than shattered plates;

it is everywhere because the present is so common;
commonly reborn,

I remember those days of sitting in a wicker chair of spilled milk
just ....listening..........

I never liked to tonsil
though my eyes did loaf   and lean among a valley of portraits;

the children weave rare wings
sprouting feathers from their shoulder-blades;

so untepid, these things—   they were the actual Actual—

star-choking and nuclear afterbirth
of the annual wooden supernova
building Mulitverses and compiling slate
and rocks with droplets of water within;

yes, this;   yes, this;

forthcoming and frothcoming, you swung and mist
you swung and mystical by a long-shot;

you chugged the mist among the slighter sights;
your old polyester heart made the solace feel entrenched

but now the rampant radiation
        and broken-winged butterflies

can finally skim the scum off the water and faces;
moonsuckle yourself to sleep— a candy made of Thought;

usually we eat fossils instead of the moon
because they are easier to come by— sometimes we drink a cloud
at night for dessert;

yes, this;   yes, this;

let the cocoons and petals flood open in the grand notion
that something so verdant, however mangled, is still here—

yes, this;   yes, this;

Electrical Juice

Pigeon wings hang in the dusty blood-dripping air;
they dangle flutterless, dead from the wires of the powerlines—

the electric crucifixes of suburbia—

a quaint sacrifice of the wide religion in a swarming town;
suspended now; heart only half a heart,

those flying things met spontaneous death;

the giants of the past were tiny and mere—

"how can you live like this?" whistled through the breeze;

the bird slumped motionless, hanging
over the street as the crackle
of intermittent voltage continued;

chaos and interruption reigned; pressed on the day
with their heavy clamor so dense that, having nowhere else to go,
grew into the sky, disrupting the navigation of airborne things—
things once magnanimous and immune
now subject to cloaked impiety— the bird slumped, as in half,
hanging, dangling on the wire above the street
as that crackle of intermittent voltage carried on;

Perishable

Sitting under cement trees
wrapped in the blissful numb;

I chose the songs
left in the space between the trough
and entrails; walking the sky
with my fingers;

toddlers of the air; I rose
to feel the grass-stains
under my back; they were purple
as a tilting cup of grape juice;

this trunk must be hollow,
I said, watching a squirrel emerge
with cheeks bloated to acorn-width;
I looked into the black hole;

saw children keeping names;
jumping through ropes;
the smell of melted plums came
and I ate their essence off the concrete
slowly turned brown through years of wood;

Alabaster Night

Bleed the day throughout;
suffer the night's
murderous whispers;

rhapsodize to yourself
in your solitude;
for to have noticed
that every second
is an eternity,
these afflictions
are made less stressful;

sundogs in the sky
are like any other gleaming:
some kind of reflected,
refracted light
through atomic crystals
among the wasteland;

Januarium

Crushed ice; now almost vaporous;
I fell into a slot of weekend;
this is such a mere relief; for the insult
will be Monday-waiting; my soul
tarnished; they've pounded my spirit
into something of a thin mist;
cold even in my only solace; I wonder
what kind of mush my nerves
and braincyst have become;

Build Your Own Cage

A mind in flux; the flux of being bored and violent;
the violence of boredom; the volatility of the bland suburbs;
in pieces; severed bushfingers taken by the thick metal clippers;
the purebred human breaks the silence
with a latent bestial roar of the frustration
from being trapped in this dull grassy cage;
shoot down the sun;
roar so loud that it wakes
the accidental mithroditist five blocks away;

there is nothing; there is no foreseeable light
anywhere ahead in this fogclad boat
of the mind; nothingseen; bothered by blindspotten vision;
in water, on land, everything is dangerous and predatory;
we live among this earthen savagery;
manmade toxins drifting up into
the nightsky causing a toxic florescence of space;
everything seems meant to kill; a long list of weapons;
pesticides and pistols; drones; spiderbites;

people went to the suburbs to escape these various dangers;
to go to a nice peaceful place as far as possible from the violence
of the world by choppingdown massive mega-acres of forest
only to find they've locked themselves in; given up their freedoms
for a false sense of security; they've made their beds
and built their own shackles that now anchor them to this place;
but as generations pass the patience wanes more so and more so;
eventually that sanctuary sought becomes rife with violence and repression;
a need to scream in the name of violence among these suburban streets;
is what's dealt here in these grassy cages;
the cork has blown off of the bottle
unleashing the latent violence;

The Ghosts of Trees

The continuance of the zabba zabba swingswirl of the Immaculate Spiral
spinning in the zula zula millenniums of light;
the coma coma awakened in you the Truth of the Spiral;
the hooli hooli zeba zeba of the contortion's twirling
spindthrift shattering the perfectly circular cage of lies
with its gola gola flood of purity pouring itself
over our bodies like milk in a yazu yazu Springtime of heart
bringing forth the bees and tulips among this chroma chroma endorphin rush;

you are quickly snapped out of the dream and brought back to the burn;

Sourly Slung

Something just ran palpable
from a ruffled Springtime; dark windy cold
encloses the Bloom; and where do we go from here?—
doubtlessly sobs will ring; sorrowed pangs
felt thick everywhere there was a wish for redemption; another try; but No;
this Spring has been a stillborn;
no vegetables reared; not a petal turned florid;
only regret of wearing such light clothes; basking
so soon in these evanescent trifles of friendly Day—
that Emptiness; that Nothingness; will reclaim its stranglehold,
sprouting wicked meagers;

Heaviest Night

Tawdry houses
drench by the sidewalk;
our liquid egg fry
forever; golden husk;
this summer is full of sweat;
came humid; unexpected
from cooler places;
we now drive [cops everywhere];
windows down; drunk in the day;
still pouring that saltine liquid
from our faces; even night
breeds dense panting [no respite]
among this house made of thick
Augustair;

Don't Take Guff from Swine

"Bad waves of visions," said the crazyman in the book;
eyes drugfilled; red-striped like candycane; his face contorted on the cover;
a flash of vegas with evil bats and cacti;
this is my own fear and I'll sow my own loathing;
smashing firefly torsos on the front porch;
painting my face with their luminous luciferin; it burns
the edge of my iris; wild green rooks; crooks;

the funnel and the vein—

I've got funerals in my veins!;

The Fake Sound of It

I came through the veil
to walk side by side with desperation;
doubtful all along the way;

I turned looking for the path's plethora of shade;
you said you'd show it to me; for my alabaster head,
my pallid newborn head, was too delicate

for the lengthy cuss the noontime sun would spit
upon it in heavy shafts from high; you said that I should
seek shelter before my innocence was assaulted;

I listened to you and at first
almost believed in it;
the fake sound of it;
the Compassion in your voice;

The Blight's Continuity

The children's parade comes to an end;
met with lava rivers up to the teeth;
melted enamel and evaporated gums;
hot liquefied jawbone; a new river;
a river of the future burning down
the Manmade aisles and passageways;
the culmination of all your sex and semen washed away,
soon to give rebirth
to the barrenness of a newborn desert;

Self-Inflicted Opprobrium

The hands cut themselves off
for stealing; this is what is known as
self-sadism; with a wrack of guilt
and no other choice, it is done
with a sharp sliver of the butcherknife;

prickly screamable; the Dog Rose
makes its midnight moonblooming;
sire of fortune and karma rolls out rose-red blood,
selfsevered, to spill forth its sanguine ejaculate upon the world;

seeds sprayed from the wrist
of the hand that cut itself off;
like eating your face; paying no attention to the parameters
defined by Proximity; a crimson lake on the floor;

Outsouled

Infected yard of spilled paint
putting forth that awkward disease
for decoration [wishes of invisibility
are invisible]; passerby stares
at my glorious mutation, vexed;
so naked, I, in that instant;
haughty king of the ugly fragile contrast
shining in the luster of most sour lime;
I pointed my finger right back
and said, "my plague, my plague, and love!";

Vanishing Summer

None tonight; euphony drifted off
with summer; the streets are strewn
with Manmade lanterns now; no more
luciferin to flicker among the night's air;
our warm nightlights are lost;
we are left only to scream
ourselves to sleep;

ABOUT THE AUTHOR

Heath Brougher lives in York, PA and attended Temple University. He is the co-poetry editor of *Into the Void Magazine*, winner of the 2017 Saboteur Award for Best Magazine after only four issues. He is a multiple Pushcart Prize and Best of the Net Nominee and his work has been translated into journals in Albania and Kosovo. He was the judge of *Into the Void's* 2016 Poetry Competition and edited the anthology *Luminous Echoes*, the proceeds of which will be donated to Pieta House in Ireland, an organization which helps prevent suicide/self-harm. He has previously published three chapbooks *A Curmudgeon is Born* (Yellow Chair Press), *Digging for Fire* and *Your Noisy Eyes* (both published by Stay Weird and Keep Writing Press) as well as one full length *About Consciousness* (Alien Buddha Press). When not writing, Brougher helps with the charity Paws Soup Kitchen which gives out free dog/cat food to low income families with pets.

ACKNOWLEDGEMENTS

"The Vulture's Grandiosity,"; "Alice in Etherland"; "Spin Now Around" and "Self-Inflicted Opprobrium" originally appeared in *Of/ with: journal of immanent renditions.*

"Applepicker's Disease" and "Chickenpox at the Slaughterhouse" originally appeared in *Five 2 One Magazine.*

"A Man Named Child" and "A Plushen World" originally appeared in *Carnival Literary Magazine.*

"Year of the Pinata" originally appeared in *Riprap Literary Journal.*

"Summer's Mechanical Thunderstorm" originally appeared in *Picaroon Poetry.*

"The United States of Anhedonia"; "Electrical Juice" and "The Deadbody Lights" originally appeared in *Otoliths* with "Electrical Juice" reposted as a Featured Poem at *Creative Talents Unleashed.*

"The Beauty of the Clusterfuck" originally appeared in *Lotus-Eater Magazine.*

"Chade in Mina" originally appeared in *Nuclear Impact Anthology.*

"Gelatinous" originally appeared in *Expound Journal.*

"Nuclear Baby" originally appeared in *SLAB Literary Magazine.*

"Bloodletting Go" originally appeared in *Chiron Review.*

"Sarin Gas for the Soul" originally appeared in *Dissident Voice.*

"The January House Colossal" originally appeared in *Fauna Quarterly.*

"Descent into Night" originally appeared in *Ink in Thirds.*

"Napalm Wig" originally appeared in *Foliate Oak*.

"Wordless" originally appeared in *No Tribal Dance Pamphlet*.

"Opus of the Opening Wounds" originally appeared in *The Bitchin' Kitsch*.

"Professional Suffering" originally appeared in *Oddball Magazine*.

"A Nightmare in Purple" originally appeared in *The Mind[less] Muse*.

"Firewater Fiend" originally appeared in *Clockwise Cat*.

"A Husk of Evening" originally appeared in *Gold Dust Magazine*.

"A Brief Respite for Remembrance" originally appeared in *Epigraph Magazine*.

"Perishable" originally appeared in *Fauna Quarterly* and was reprinted in *Tipton Poetry Journal*.

"Alabaster Night" originally appeared in *Blue Mountain Review*.

"Januarium" originally appeared in *Between These Shores*.

"The Ghosts of Trees" originally appeared in *The Jawline Review*.

"Sourly Slung" and "Heaviest Night" originally appeared in *Section 8 Magazine*.

"Don't Take Guff from Swine" originally appeared in *Stay Weird and Keep Writing Co.*

"The Fake Sound of It" originally appeared in *eFiction India*.

"The Blight's Continuity" originally appeared in *Fowl Fox Review*.

"Outsouled" originally appeared in *BlazeVOX*.

"Vanishing Summer" originally appeared in *Napalm and Novocain*.

Made in the USA
Monee, IL
26 March 2021